# MATCH
## with Clifford
### THE BIG RED DOG®

• • • • • • • • • • • • • • • • • • • • • • • • • • • • • •

**Activities for Building
Fine-Motor Skills and Teaching Basic Concepts**

**■SCHOLASTIC**

New York • Toronto • London • Auckland • Sydney
Mexico City • New Delhi • Hong Kong • Buenos Aires

FREE Activity Book Online!
Go to teacherexpress.scholastic.com/Clifford

Originally published as *Little Kids . . . Match!*
Cover design by Michelle Kim
Written and illustrated by Karen Sevaly

ISBN: 978-0-545-81963-3
Copyright © 2015 by Scholastic Inc.
All rights reserved. Published by Scholastic Inc.
Printed in China.

1 2 3 4 5 6 7 8 9 10   68   21 20 19 18 17 16 15

# Contents

**W**elcome to the wonderful world of young learners, where learning is like play with everyone's much-loved canine—Clifford The Big Red Dog®! This book offers easy activities that will help your child develop the skills needed to meet key early curriculum standards and succeed in school. The activities provide practice in sorting and classifying objects that are alike and different, sequencing, counting, copying simple patterns, learning basic concepts, and more.

Each activity page targets specific skills for your child to practice. The consistent format will help your child work independently and with self-assurance. Other important features include:

- easy-to-follow directions to help build vocabulary, as well as math and early reading comprehension skills

- matching and cut-and-paste exercises to develop and strengthen your child's visual discrimination, eye-hand coordination, and fine-motor skills

- appealing artwork that engages and motivates your child to learn

On the following pages, you'll find suggestions for introducing the activity pages to your child, tips for getting started and making the experience go smoothly, plus activities you can do with your child to extend learning.

We hope you and your child enjoy doing the activities in this book. Your involvement will help make this a valuable educational experience and will support and enhance your child's learning. And with Clifford The Big Red Dog® along for company, it's sure to be filled with fun!

## What's Inside

Most young children naturally begin expressing mathematical concepts as they discover the world around them. Young learners also need the opportunity to classify objects, identify simple patterns, and begin using language to communicate their thinking. These skills are essential to the understanding of mathematical concepts and problem solving. The activities in this book have been designed for the developmental abilities of your young child. The big, bold pictures and thick cutting lines offer support as your child practices matching, sorting and classifying, and other skills. These features let your child experience success, helping build self-esteem and confidence. Here's a look at the different kinds of activities in this book.

**Picture Match** (pages 7 and 8)
In these beginning activities, your child uses visual discrimination skills to match pictures that are the same.

*Match With Clifford The Big Red Dog®* © Scholastic Inc.

### Go-Together Pictures (pages 9–11)

On these pages, your child identifies and groups together pictures that share common characteristics.

### Same and Different (pages 12–16)

To further develop visual discrimination skills, your child identifies the object in a group that is different from the others. The exercises increase in challenge on pages 15 and 16.

### Basic Concepts (pages 17–23)

These activities give your child practice in sorting and classifying objects according to size (e.g., big/little, same size, smallest/largest, short/tall), and position (e.g., up/down, in/out).

### Sequence a Story (pages 24 and 25)

To help build both early math and reading skills, your child studies the scrambled pictures that tell a wordless story, and then numbers the pages to put the events of the story in the correct order. Guide your child by asking questions, such as *What happens first*? *What happens next*? *Then what happens*? and *What happens at the end*?

### Count and Match (pages 26–28)

On these pages, your child counts and matches sets that have the same number of objects.

### Position Picture Puzzles (pages 29–35)

For more practice with concepts that describe position (front/back and top/middle/bottom), your child colors, then cuts apart and reassembles simple puzzles. After completing the puzzles, your child may enjoy pasting them to sheets of construction paper.

## Helpful Tips

- For ease of use, simply choose the skills you would like your child to work on (you'll find detailed information on the Contents page), locate the corresponding activity page in the book, and gently tear out the page along the perforated edges.

- The only materials needed for the activities are crayons or pencils, child-safe scissors, and glue or glue sticks.

- Help your child read the directions on the activity pages.

- Let your child complete each activity page at his or her own pace.

- Review the completed pages together and encourage your child to share the thinking behind his or her responses.

- Support your child's efforts and offer help when needed.

- Display your child's work and share his or her progress with family and friends!

**Copy the Pattern** (pages 37–41)
To practice recognizing patterns, an important early math skill, your child cuts out and pastes pictures to recreate a given pattern.

**Match, Paste, and Color** (pages 43 and 45)
These fun exercises invite your child to match and put together puzzle pieces to form a picture.

**Achievement Certificates** (page 47)
After your child has completed the activity pages, acknowledge his or her efforts by completing the "I Can Match Pictures!" and "I Can Count & Match!" certificates. Post them on the refrigerator or on a bulletin board to honor your child's achievements.

## Extending Learning
Here are a few ideas to give your child more practice developing matching skills.

### Alike and Different
Name or show your child two objects, such as a fork and a spoon. Ask him or her to think of ways the two objects are similar and ways in which they are different. You might also select several everyday objects that go together and one object that is different, for example, three socks and one shoe; or a pencil, a pen, a crayon, and a cup. Ask your child to identify the object that doesn't belong.

### Pasta Sort and Match
Give your child a muffin tin and a few pieces of several different types of dry pasta (e.g., elbows, shells, bow ties, and wheels). Discuss how the shapes and sizes are alike and different. Then have your child sort each type of pasta into a separate muffin cup. You might repeat this activity with other items, such as different types of dry cereal.

### Sequence Stories
After reading a favorite story, discuss with your child the events that make up the beginning, middle, and end. Or, after reading a comic strip from the newspaper, create sequence cards by cutting up the strip and helping your child put the pictures back in order.

### Color Patterns
Use red and black checkers, blue and red poker chips, or colored, plastic manipulatives to help your child practice making a pattern. Start by asking your child to sort the objects by color. Next, arrange a pattern of alternating colors, such as blue/red/blue/red, and ask your child to continue the pattern. Eventually, introduce other kinds of patterns for your child to practice. Also invite your child to make up his or her own patterns!

# Picture Match Look at the pictures on this page.
## Draw a line to connect the matching pictures.

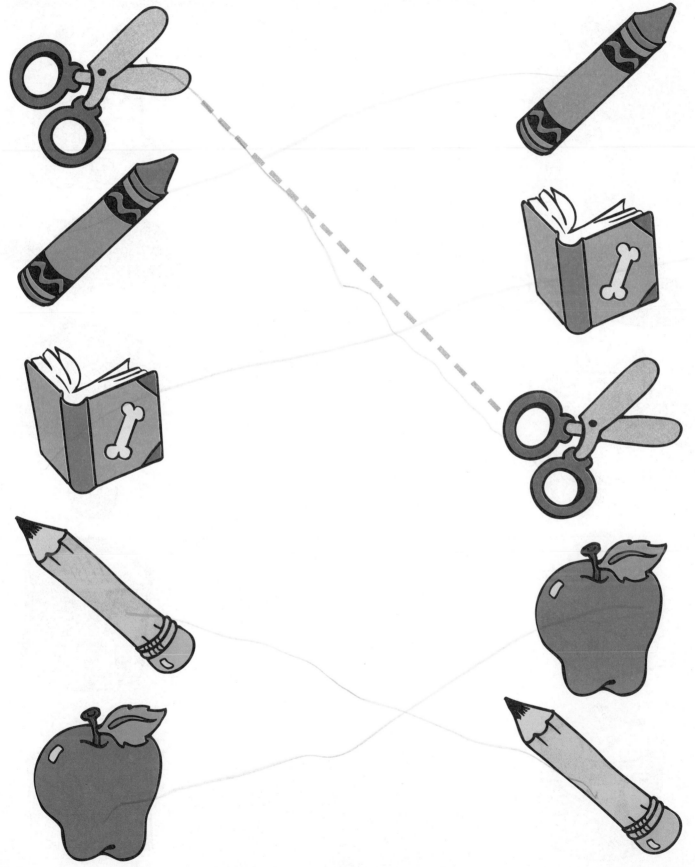

# Picture Match Look at the pictures on this page.
## Draw a line to connect the matching pictures.

# Go-Together Pictures Look at the pictures in each box.
## Circle the pictures that go together.

## Go-Together Pictures Look at the pictures in each box. Circle the pictures that go together.

# Go-Together Pictures Look at the pictures in each box.
## Circle the pictures that go together.

# Same and Different Look at the pictures in each row.
## Circle the pictures that are the same.
## Put an X on the picture that is different.

# Same and Different Look at the pictures in each row. Circle the pictures that are the same. Put an X on the picture that is different.

*Match With Clifford The Big Red Dog®* © Scholastic Inc.

**Same and Different** Look at the pictures in each row.
Circle the pictures that are the same.
Put an X on the picture that is different.

# Same and Different Look at the pictures in each row. Circle the picture that is different from the others.

# Same and Different Look at the pictures in each row. Circle the picture that is different from the others.

# Big and Little Look at the pictures in each box.
## Circle the big picture. Put an X on the little picture.

*Match With Clifford The Big Red Dog* © Scholastic Inc.

# Same Size Look at the pictures in each row.
# Circle the pictures that are the same size.

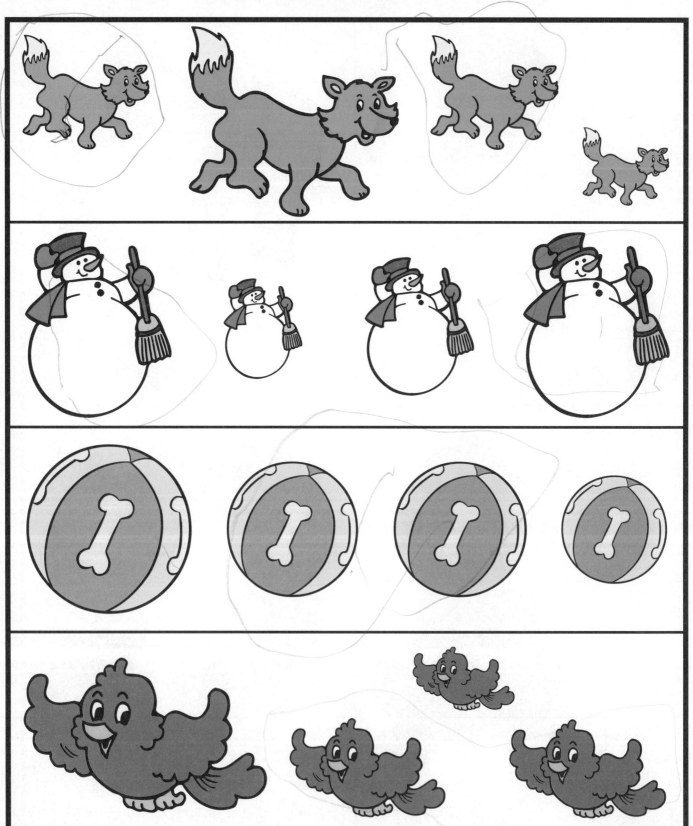

# Same Size Look at the pictures in each row.
## Circle the pictures that are the same size.

# Smallest and Largest Look at the pictures in each box. Circle the smallest picture. Put an X on the largest.

# Short and Tall Look at the pictures in each box.
Circle the short picture. Put an X on the tall picture.

# Up and Down Look at the pictures in each box.
## Circle the up picture. Put an X on the down picture.

# In and Out Look at the pictures in each box.
## Circle the in picture. Put an X on the out picture.

**Sequence a Story Number these pictures in the order that they happen.**

# Sequence a Story Number these pictures in the order that they happen.

# Count and Match Draw a line to connect the sets that have the same number of objects.

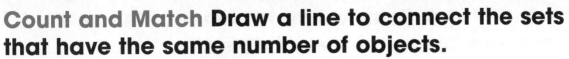

# Count and Match Draw a line to connect the sets that have the same number of objects.

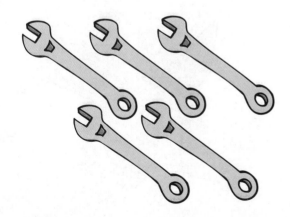

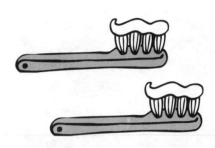

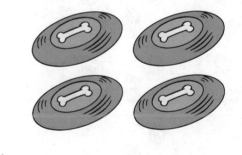

# Count and Match Draw a line to connect the sets that have the same number of objects.

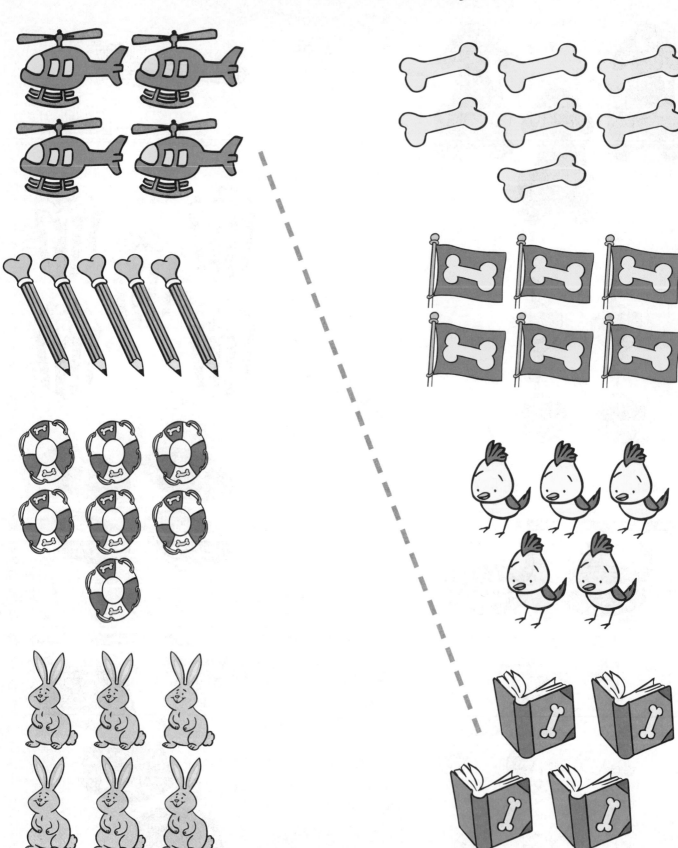

*Match With Clifford The Big Red Dog® © Scholastic Inc.*

# Front and Back Color these pictures. Cut them out along the bold, black lines. Put the pieces back together.

**Top, Middle, and Bottom Color these pictures. Cut them out along the bold, black lines. Put the pieces back together.**

*Match With Clifford The Big Red Dog*® © Scholastic Inc.

**Top, Middle, and Bottom** Color these pictures. Cut them out along the bold, black lines. Put the pieces back together.

**Clown's Face** Color this clown's face. Cut it apart along the bold, black lines. Put the pieces back together.

# Copy the Pattern Look at the pattern below.
## Cut and paste the pictures at the bottom of the page in the same order.

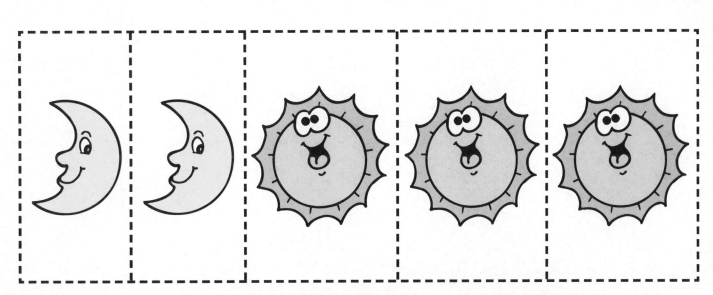

# Copy the Pattern Look at the pattern below.
## Cut and paste the pictures at the bottom of the page in the same order.

# Copy the Pattern Look at the pattern below.
## Cut and paste the pictures at the bottom of the page in the same order.

**Match, Paste, and Color** Cut out the puzzle pieces along the bold, black lines. Put them together to form a picture, then paste and color. What did you make?

**Match, Paste, and Color** Cut out the puzzle pieces along the bold, black lines. Put them together to form a picture, then paste and color. What did you make?

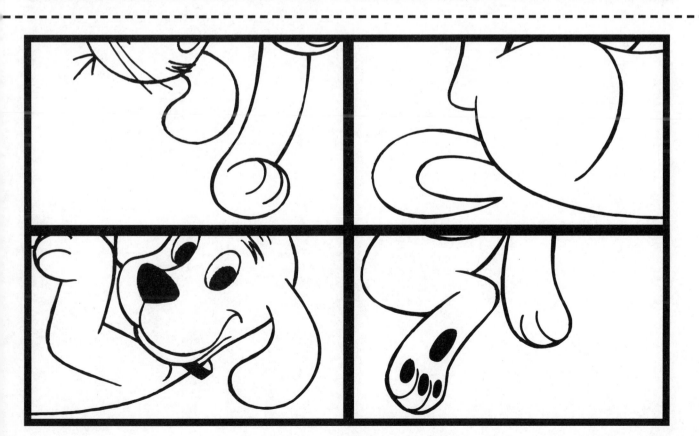

Awesome!

Way To Go!

# I Can Match Pictures!

Great Job!

Excellent!

_____
Name

_____
Parent

_____
Date

# I Can Count & Match!

_____
Name

_____
Parent

_____
Date